W9-CLM-696

Arctic Foxes

by Carri Stuhr

Lerner Publications Company • Minneapolis

For Nathan and Carson

The images in this book are used with the permission of: © iStockphoto.com/Dimitry Deshevykh, pp. 4, 39, 47; © Laura Westlund/Independent Picture Service, p. 5; © Maria Stenzel/National Geographic/Getty Images, p. 6; © Chris Schenk/Foto Natura/Minden Pictures/Getty Images, p. 7; © Bernd Geh/Photographer's Choice/Getty Images, p. 8; © Wayne Lynch/DRK PHOTO, p. 9; © Steve Kazlowski/Danita Delimont Agency/drr.net, pp. 10, 34, 48 (top); © Matthias Breiter/Minden Pictures/Getty Images, pp. 11, 16; © Yva Momatiuk/John Eastcott/Minden Pictures/Getty Images, p. 12; © Johnny Johnson/Photographer's Choice/ Getty Images, p. 13; © SuperStock, Inc./SuperStock, p. 14; © age fotostock/SuperStock, p. 15; © James Hager/Robert Harding World Imagery/Getty Images, p. 17; © Paul Nicklen/ National Geographic/Getty Images, p. 18; © Stephen J. Krasemann/DRK PHOTO, p. 19; © Norbert Rosing/National Geographic/Getty Images, pp. 20, 30; © Randy Green/drr.net, p. 21; © Jordi Bas Casas/NHPA/Photoshot, p. 22; © Norbert Rosing/Photolibrary/Getty Images, p. 23; © Natphotos/Photodisc/Getty Images, p. 24; © WILDLIFE/Peter Arnold, Inc., p. 25; © Thomas Schmitt/Photographer's Choice/Getty Images, p. 26; © Randy Green/Taxi/ Getty Images, p. 27; © Alan Carey/Photo Researchers, Inc., p. 28; © Johnny Johnson/Animals Animals, p. 29; © Theo Allofs/Riser/Getty Images, p. 31; © Michio Hoshino/Minden Pictures/ Getty Images, p. 32; © Arthur Morris/Visuals Unlimited, p. 33; © Steven Kazlowski/Science Faction/Getty Images, p. 35; © Bryan & Cherry Alexander Photography/Alamy, p. 36; © Sean Gallup/Getty Images, p. 37; © Arctic-Images/Iconica/Getty Images, p. 38; © Joel W. Rogers/ CORBIS, pp. 40, 41, 42; © Imagebroker/Alamy, p. 43; © Purestock/Getty Images, p. 46; © Tom Ulrich/Visuals Unlimited, p. 48 (bottom).

Cover: © David W. Hamilton/The Image Bank/Getty Images.

Lerner Publications Company
A division of Lerner Publishing Group, Inc.
241 First Avenue North
Minneapolis, MN 55401 U.S.A.

Website address: www.lernerbooks.com

Library of Congress Cataloging-in-Publication Data

Stuhr, Carri.
    Arctic foxes / by Carri Stuhr.
        p.   cm. — (Early bird nature books)
    Includes index.
    ISBN 978–0–8225–9432–1 (lib. bdg. : alk. paper)
    1. Arctic fox—Juvenile literature. I. Title.
QL737.C22S79 2009
599.775—dc22   2008022051

Manufactured in the United States of America
1 2 3 4 5 6 – BP – 14 13 12 11 10 09

Contents

Arctic foxes can be found in the northern parts of Alaska and Canada and in Greenland. The yellow areas show where arctic foxes live.

Be a Word Detective

Can you find these words as you read about the arctic fox's life? Be a detective and try to figure out what they mean. You can turn to the glossary on page 46 for help.

arctic
caches
camouflage
dens
environment

global warming
lemming
litter
molt
permafrost

predators
pups
radio collars
scavengers
species
territory

Chapter 1

This arctic fox is hiding in the snow. Do you know where arctic foxes live?

The Arctic Fox

Two eyes and a nose poke out of the snow. This furry face belongs to an arctic fox. The arctic fox can hide in the snow because it has white fur.

The arctic fox makes its home in the arctic. This is how the animal gets its name. The arctic is a part of Earth that is far north. It includes the North Pole and the Arctic Ocean. The arctic also includes land in North America, Europe, and Asia.

This arctic fox lives in the far north of Canada. This part of North America is in the arctic.

The arctic is covered with snow for most of the year.

The arctic is very cold. In the winter, ice
and snow cover the land. In some parts of the
arctic, the ground stays frozen all year long.
The frozen layer of soil is called permafrost.

Arctic foxes are ready for the cold weather. They have a thick coat of fur. Their fur keeps them warm when the temperature drops.

Arctic foxes even have fur on the bottoms of their feet! The fur acts like a pair of warm boots. It protects a fox's feet as it walks across the ice.

This is the front paw of an arctic fox. It is covered with fur. This fur protects the fox from the ice when it walks.

The arctic fox has small, rounded ears. It has short legs too. These body parts help the fox keep heat close to its body. They help it to stay warm in the arctic.

Arctic foxes are built for cold weather. They also have bushy tails that can cover them to help keep them warm.

In the winter, arctic foxes (left) *have white fur so they blend into the snow. This makes it hard for enemies to see them. Red foxes* (right) *don't blend into the snow.*

The arctic fox's coloring also helps it to survive in the arctic. In the winter, most arctic foxes grow a coat of white fur. This white fur acts as camouflage (KAM-oh-flahzh) in the snow. The fox's coloring helps it blend into its surroundings. The fur helps arctic foxes hide from other animals.

This blue fox lives on an island off the coast of Alaska.

Some arctic foxes turn gray with a hint of blue in the winter. These foxes are sometimes called blue foxes. The blue foxes live close to the water.

In the spring, arctic foxes molt. This means they shed their fur. New fur grows in its place. The new fur is brown. It's also short. The lighter coat keeps arctic foxes cool in summer months.

Arctic foxes lose their warm winter fur in the spring. In the summer, their fur is darker and thinner.

Arctic foxes are members of the dog family.
The dog family includes wolves, coyotes, jackals,
and the dogs you see in your neighborhood.

*This golden retriever is related to arctic foxes. They
are all part of the dog family.*

Like other dogs, arctic foxes have strong teeth. These teeth are for eating meat.

The dog family has strong teeth for eating meat. Members of the dog family also have good hearing and a good sense of smell. These strong senses help them find food and avoid danger.

The arctic fox is one of 21 species (SPEE-sheez) of foxes. A species is a group of plants or animals that have similar features. The largest fox species is the red fox. The red fox is well known in North America and Europe.

The arctic fox is much smaller than the red fox. The arctic fox weighs only about 6 to 10 pounds (2.7 to 4.5 kilograms). That is about the size of a cat.

An arctic fox and a red fox search for food in the arctic tundra.

Chapter 2

This arctic fox is looking for food. What do arctic foxes eat?

Arctic Fox Food

Arctic foxes are always looking for food. A fox might travel near the water to eat seabirds, seabird eggs, baby seals, and fish. Foxes also sometimes snack on grass and berries. These foods grow in the arctic during the summer.

The lemming is the main food source for an arctic fox. Lemmings are little animals that look like mice. They have small, furry bodies and short tails.

A lemming walks across snow. Arctic foxes hunt lemmings for food.

An arctic fox pounces on a lemming under the snow.

Lemmings hide in tunnels under the snow. The arctic fox listens for the lemmings as they move through the tunnels. When the fox hears a lemming, it jumps up and down to break the snow. Then it pounces on the lemming to kill it.

This arctic fox caught something to eat.

Arctic foxes are good hunters. They are also clever scavengers (SKAV-uhn-jurz). A scavenger eats dead animals. An arctic fox is too small to kill a walrus or a caribou. But a fox will eat a dead walrus or caribou it finds while traveling across the arctic.

Arctic foxes also follow polar bears to get meat. Polar bears kill many animals for their meat. Arctic foxes wait for polar bears to eat their catch. When the polar bear is done, the arctic fox will eat the leftovers!

Arctic foxes sometimes follow polar bears. The fox waits and then steals some of the bear's catch.

Arctic foxes have plenty of food in the summer. A fox may even have extra food. Arctic foxes store extra food in caches (KASHes). A cache is a hiding spot. In the winter, it can be hard to find food. If the foxes get hungry in the winter, they can dig up the food they stored in the summer.

During the summer, foxes can snack on grass and berries. They often store food in the summer for the long winter ahead.

Chapter 3

Arctic foxes live in groups in the summer. Do they live in groups in the winter?

Arctic Fox Groups

Arctic foxes live and hunt in small groups in the spring and summer. This group includes a male, a female, and several children. The foxes separate at the end of summer. The male and female come back together in the spring.

Some fox groups live in small areas when there is plenty of food.

The area where a group of arctic foxes lives and hunts is called a territory (TAYR-uh-tohr-ee). Some fox groups have small territories. These foxes live in areas with plenty of food. They don't need to spread out to hunt.

Other fox groups have large territories.
These foxes live in places where food is harder
to find. They must travel to do their hunting.

*Some territories have little food. Foxes in these
territories have to travel more to find enough to eat.*

Arctic foxes bark to find one another in their territories. One fox calls out with a bark. The other foxes answer. The foxes exchange barks until they meet.

These arctic foxes are listening. Foxes bark to find other members of their group.

This arctic fox is prepared for danger. Foxes bark to warn other foxes of danger.

Arctic foxes also bark to warn one another of danger. This bark is loud and high. It tells the other foxes to run and hide.

Chapter 4

An arctic fox mother and her babies look around near their home. What are arctic fox babies called?

Young Arctic Foxes

Baby arctic foxes are born in early summer. Baby foxes are called cubs, kits, or pups.

Baby arctic foxes are born in dens.
Dens are safe places. Some are deep holes
underground. Others are tunnels dug in piles
of rocks or wood.

These arctic fox cubs live in a den underneath some logs.

Many baby foxes are born at once. A mother fox may have more than 10 babies. A group of baby foxes is called a litter.

The babies in the litter are helpless at first. They cannot see or hear. Both parents help raise the babies.

This litter of baby foxes has at least 6 babies. Sometimes litters have more than 10 babies.

This arctic fox is carrying food back to its den. Both mother and father arctic foxes feed their babies.

For the first few weeks, the babies drink their mother's milk. The father goes out hunting and brings food to the den.

After three weeks in the den, the young foxes are ready to explore. At first, the babies stay close to home. In a few months, they are ready to travel farther. Their parents teach them how to hunt.

Arctic fox pups play with one another.

When arctic fox babies are old enough, they will live by themselves. The next spring, they will start a new family.

The babies leave their parents before winter arrives. They are old enough to live on their own. They live and hunt by themselves for a while. Then they are ready to start their own families.

Chapter 5

This is a wolverine. Wolverines eat arctic foxes. What other animals eat arctic foxes?

Dangers for Arctic Foxes

The arctic fox has enemies in the wild. Golden eagles, polar bears, and wolverines will eat arctic foxes. These animals are predators (PREH-duh-turz). Predators are animals that hunt and eat other animals.

The arctic fox has other animal predators too. Owls and wolves hunt arctic foxes. A wolf will eat an arctic fox for a snack!

This is a snowy owl. Snowy owls sometimes eat arctic fox pups.

People are another danger for the arctic fox. People hunt arctic foxes for their fur. They use the fur to make coats, hats, and mittens.

Some people hunt arctic foxes for money. They sell the fur to people who make clothing for cold weather.

*Many factories release dirty gases into the air.
These gases hurt the environment.*

Hunting isn't the only way that people harm the arctic fox. They also harm the animal by hurting its environment. People drive cars that release gases. They run factories that release gases, too.

Gases put in the air affect the temperature of the arctic.

Scientists say that these gases are changing Earth's temperature. The gases are making Earth slowly grow warmer. The slow rise in Earth's temperature is known as global warming.

Global warming causes some animals to leave their homes. They move to places with cooler temperatures. The red fox is one such animal. It has moved into the arctic foxes' home.

Red foxes are much bigger than arctic foxes. They take over arctic foxes' dens. They eat arctic foxes' food. This hurts the arctic fox.

Red foxes have moved into the same area that arctic foxes live in. Arctic foxes then have to fight red foxes for food.

Scientists want to help the arctic fox. They study the animal to learn more about it. This way, the scientists will know how to help it.

These markings in the snow are arctic fox footprints. Scientists find arctic foxes by tracking the footprints back to the fox.

This scientist is studying the arctic fox. The fox was given a shot so it would stay still.

Scientists study the arctic fox by tracking it. They attach tags to certain foxes' ears. The tags help scientists keep track of these foxes. Then the scientists can study the foxes and learn how they live.

This fox is wearing a radio collar. It allows scientists to see where the fox goes.

Scientists also use radio collars to track foxes. A radio collar looks like the collar you see on a dog. The collars have special instruments in them. The instruments send signals to scientists. The scientists use the signals to find the arctic foxes.

Scientists have learned a lot about arctic foxes. Many people describe them as friendly. They are not shy around humans. They will even come close if they know you have food. You may see one if you visit the arctic. Or you can look at one at the zoo.

These arctic foxes live in a zoo in Germany.

ON SHARING A BOOK

When you share a book with a child, you show that reading is important. To get the most out of the experience, read in a comfortable, quiet place. Turn off the television and limit other distractions, such as telephone calls.

Be prepared to start slowly. Take turns reading parts of this book. Stop occasionally and discuss what you're reading. Talk about the photographs. If the child begins to lose interest, stop reading. When you pick up the book again, revisit the parts you have already read.

BE A VOCABULARY DETECTIVE

The word list on page 5 contains words that are important in understanding the topic of this book. Be word detectives and search for the words as you read the book together. Talk about what the words mean and how they are used in the sentence. Do any of these words have more than one meaning? You will find the words defined in a glossary on page 46.

WHAT ABOUT QUESTIONS?

Use questions to make sure the child understands the information in this book. Here are some suggestions:

> What did this paragraph tell us? What does this picture show? What do you think we'll learn about next? Where do arctic foxes live? What color is their fur? Could an arctic fox live in your backyard? Why or why not? What do arctic foxes eat? What is your favorite part of this book? Why?

If the child has questions, don't hesitate to respond with questions of your own, such as What do *you* think? Why? What is it that you don't know? If the child can't remember certain facts, turn to the index.

INTRODUCING THE INDEX

The index helps readers find information without searching through the whole book. Turn to the index on page 48. Choose an entry such as *food*, and ask the child to use the index to find out what the arctic fox's main food source is. Repeat this exercise with as many entries as you like. Ask the child to point out the differences between an index and a glossary. (The index helps readers find information, while the glossary tells readers what words mean.)

LEARN MORE ABOUT
ARCTIC FOXES

BOOKS

Alexander, Bryan, and Cherry Alexander. *Journey into the Arctic*. New York: Oxford University Press USA, 2003. Find out about the animals and people that live in the arctic.

DuTemple, Lesley A. *Polar Bears*. Minneapolis: Lerner Publications Company, 1997. Read about the polar bear, which also lives in the arctic.

Glassman, Jackie. *Amazing Arctic Animals*. New York: Grosset & Dunlap, 2002. Learn more about the arctic and the animals that live there, including arctic foxes.

Person, Stephen. *Arctic Fox: Very Cool!* New York: Bearport Publishing Company, 2008. Find out more about the arctic fox and its home in the arctic.

WEBSITES

Arctic Studies Center
http://www.mnh.si.edu/arctic/html/arctic_fox.html
This site has useful information about the arctic fox and other arctic animals.

CyberZoo: Arctic Fox
http://lsb.syr.edu/projects/cyberzoo/arcticfox.html
Visit this site to learn more about the arctic fox. The site includes a drawing of an arctic fox food web.

GLOSSARY

arctic: a part of Earth that is far north. The arctic includes the North Pole, the Arctic Ocean, and parts of North America, Europe, and Asia.

caches (KASHes): hiding spots for food

camouflage (KAM-oh-flahzh): coloring that helps an animal blend into its surroundings and hide

dens: safe places where foxes live and baby foxes are born. A fox den could be a deep hole underground or a tunnel dug in a pile of rocks or wood.

environment: the place where an animal lives. Air, soil, weather, plants, and animals are all part of the environment.

global warming: the slow rise in Earth's temperature

lemming: the main food source for an arctic fox. Lemmings are little animals that look like mice.

litter: a group of baby foxes that is born to one mother

molt: to shed

permafrost: a layer of ground that stays frozen all year

predators (PREH-duh-turz): animals that hunt and eat other animals

pups: a name for baby arctic foxes. Baby arctic foxes are also called cubs or kits.

radio collars: collars used to track wild animals

scavengers (SKAV-uhn-jurz): animals that eat dead animals

species (SPEE-sheez): a group of plants or animals that have similar features

territory (TAYR-uh-tohr-ee): the area where a group of arctic foxes lives and hunts

INDEX

Pages listed in **bold** type refer to photographs.